ROOMS A

WICK POETRY FIRST BOOK SERIES
Maggie Anderson, Editor

Already the World
Victoria Redel   Gerald Stern, Judge

Likely
Lisa Coffman   Alicia Suskin Ostriker, Judge

Intended Place
Rosemary Willey   Yusef Komunyakaa, Judge

The Apprentice of Fever
Richard Tayson   Marilyn Hacker, Judge

Beyond the Velvet Curtain
Karen Kovacik   Henry Taylor, Judge

The Gospel of Barbecue
Honorée Fanonne Jeffers   Lucille Clifton, Judge

Paper Cathedrals
Morri Creech   Li-Young Lee, Judge

Back Through Interruption
Kate Northrop   Lynn Emanuel, Judge

The Drowned Girl
Eve Alexandra   C. K. Williams, Judge

Rooms and Fields: Dramatic
Monologues from the War in Bosnia
Lee Peterson   Jean Valentine, Judge

Rooms and Fields

Dramatic Monologues from the War in Bosnia

Poems by

Lee Peterson

The Kent State University Press

Kent & London

© 2004 by Lee Peterson
Library of Congress Catalog Card Number 2004007626
ISBN 0-87338-816-x
Manufactured in the United States of America

08 07 06 05 04   5 4 3 2 1

The Wick Poetry First Book Series is sponsored by the Stan and Tom Wick Poetry
Program and the Department of English at Kent State University.

Library of Congress Cataloging-in-Publication Data
Peterson, Lee 1971–
    Rooms and fields : dramatic monologues from the war in Bosnia / Lee Peterson.
        p.   cm.—(Wick poetry first book series)
    ISBN 0-87338-816-x (pbk.: alk paper)
    1. Bosnia and Hercegovina—Poetry.   2. Yugoslav War, 1991–1995—Poetry.
    3. War poetry, American.   I. Title.   II. Series.
PS3616.E843R66 2004
811'.6—dc22   2004007626

British Library Cataloging-in-Publication data are available.

CONTENTS

Right from the start, right from the subtitle, this long poem is bold and risky: *Dramatic Monologues from the War in Bosnia.* I was both awed and skeptical as I took up the first page, the second page; but almost at once I was held by Lee Peterson's authority. Here we are going to be told artistic and historical truth.

The book has a formal movement, which helps to contain (artistically) the violence and deep tragedy that is the poem's subject. There is almost infinite variety in the burden of the voices; I thought here of Brenda Hillman's beautiful line, "Every voice is needed." I thought, too, of John Berryman's early songs, like "The Song of the Tortured Girl." The voices themselves seem to me to be written in that "third language" that Anne Carson talks about as a goal for the translator: to write not in the language of the original, nor in the language of the translator, but to find a third language, ideal to the work's translation.

These poems are full of surprises: ancient authors talk; the dictionary talks; very memorably; the bridge over the Drina River, roughly between Bosnia and Serbia, speaks two haunting poems. The dead talk, wolves talk, a tyrant talks, with a chorus. Sometimes I like to imagine this long poem being staged. What would the music be! Who would do the sets! What languages . . .

Lee Peterson's *Rooms and Fields: Dramatic Monologues from the War in Bosnia* doesn't have a single wasted breath; its sense of necessity never lets up; I always feel that the people and animals and landscapes being written about are being honored. The work is compassionate and single-mindedly alive to its high purpose. What a rare thing it is to find the meeting of historical, political, and poetic wisdom. It is redemptive that chance has brought this book to be published as the Stan and Tom Wick Poetry Prize at Kent State University. And we have never needed such a poem of witness more.

NOTE TO THE READER

The names that appear below the poems' titles in italics are the names of the poems' fictional speakers. During the war in Bosnia-Herzegovina (1992–95), ethnic identity could often only be discerned by a person's name, and within this, often only by the last name. The ethnic identities of the fictional speakers in my poems are sometimes deliberately ambiguous, though most are Bosnian Muslim, as a name like "Fatima" would suggest.

Given the historical nature of the series, and the fact that the reader may not be familiar with a number of the references, the notes at the end are extensive and an integral part of the book.

Finally, a brief note on Bosnian pronunciation:

c   is *ts* as in "cats"
č   is *ch* as in "church"
ć   is similar to č, roughly *tj* as in "future"
lj is *ll* as in "million"
ś   is *sh* as in "shy"

ROOMS AND FIELDS

Don't look at us
with those eyes of yours
too widely open
like the eyes of the dead.
— Wisława Szymborska

ROOMS

THE NATIONAL LIBRARY

Sabiha

I had decided to study history at university
the day the library started burning.
I was loaded down with books on my way to my parents' house.

People darted. They jerked like fish
caught on a huge, dry stone.

I stood and watched for the longest time.
Pieces of paper lit on my shoulders and hands.
It was August, my birthday.

I'd been thinking how my mother would cry
when she saw I'd cut my hair. I'd light a cigarette. I'd wait.

I'd been thinking how to tell my father:
History, Papa. Not mathematics. Not physics.
My father mistrusted history.

I stood at the bridge preparing my speech.
The leather straps dug into my shoulders.
I stood until the fish settled on their stone

until ash gathered at my feet,
until it covered my face
and the rest of me.

COLORS

Zahid

At night in winter I would sit
by the blue and white flames of the stove
in the corner and watch my wife.

She talked about the town.
Her sister.
His son.
(I only looked to listen.)

She wore an apron with red buds
blooming across her chest.

She knit in her chair—shiny silver needles
and yellow wool.

She knit jumpers for our grandchildren,
jumpers for our neighbor's son.

PAPA'S DREAM

Fatima

I.

This year the neighbors won't bring eggs.
And the lamb we meant for Bairam
will be born still.

The ewe's pointy skull through the rails
will scan the woods for her.

II.

Mama and I tuck our hair under scarves
and wear glass charms.
While my brother, Mufid, keeps an iron blade.

In the kitchen, we speak only commands, no names.

Only
Kahva.

Only
Tiho.

III.

Papa starts awake to a white dawn,
to dew and grain and the rest of us
sleeping.

He bends to tie his shoes like every morning.
Long before ours, his day begins.

WATER

Denis

Outside, the cement cracks where it wouldn't.
We dig trenches to get to work.
Asphalt on top of asphalt on top of dirt.

I try to go at night, plastic bottles strung like lanterns
around my shoulders and thighs. Which is safer,
the dark walk at night or the sprint in day? It's a running debate.

Sanja thought ahead and filled her closets with water.
Wine bottles, milk jugs everywhere.
We still take them, one at a time.

That's how many she stored.
Much good it did her.
Blown wall. Half oven. Burned, curled wallpaper.

We take one and head to the basement
on days we wouldn't dare run
on nights the cement cracks where it wouldn't.

In the basement, everyone brings different things.
I take a book. Asim takes his makeup.
Mrs. Djurdjić brings her starving Persian.

ZLATA ON THE OUTSIDE

Rahima

Hurry, hurry.
Through
the outside.

Hurry.
From inside
to inside.

Hurry, hurry.
Hard rain
from the hills.

The outside
can catch you child.
Hurry.

MORNING

Petra

In the mists we move them through the orchard
or the fields (the long grass sharp) while my son
and his boys sleep in the hills until noon.

The strangers can't stay but to take some bread.
Then my husband and I reach a hand and hard whisper:
  God go with you. Go!

Then, like torches they light and turn.
They burn, I tell you, like stones.

BURYING TITO

Munira

Before we left our house, my mother took one set of everything
we'd need and buried it. Sheets, towels, winter clothes. I sifted
through my own piles upstairs. I helped my mother prepare the
packages—*Everything in plastic bags, two times!* Everything labeled,
everything named. At one point she left the room and went
downstairs to get more tape and bags. But when she returned I
only saw his picture in her hands. She'd grabbed him from the hall.
She was stupid to save him, I said and found a bag and labeled it.
She said, I know and laughed. We buried Tito under the house,
with the rest of our things, our disposable lives.

WOLVES

Vuk

From the first war my family
ran deep from where the sun goes.
From forest to forest.

They came here
looking for life and kill.
But now . . .

The cubs, still blind,
wail into their mother.
The bears move north.

Men pass the trees
on metal wheels and legs.
They look toward nothing I can see.

(I fear they've come for the forests.
I fear they come for us.)

Butterfly. Bird of prey.
I keep watch in the day.

THE TEACHER

Slobo (with chorus)

Your fathers have suffered
And you are their sons

    Bright futures! Dark returns!

You think you know them
That they are your friends

    Bright futures! Dark returns!

But they will steal
Your very skins

    Bright futures! Dark returns!

And crush your memories
Like your bones

    Bright futures! Dark returns!

I tell you!
You have suffered for *their* sins

    Bright futures! Dark returns!
    Bright futures! Dark returns!

CARNIVAL

Sabiha at her studies

*Odysseus, it seems, had promised Hecabe and Helen that all who offered
no resistance should be spared. Yet now the Greeks poured silently
through the moonlit streets, broke into the unguarded houses, and cut the
throats of the Trojans as they slept.*

LOVE SONG FOR IBRAHIM

Zada

Late summer
I'd bring him lunch in the field,
my Ibrahim.

The closer I came,
the wider the rows
stretched on and on.

And always
a murmur,
the rustle of stalks.

I thought but never asked:
How does it feel
to hold the wood,

to swing the blade
and swing again
Ibrahim?

Does it become your body?
Your body the corn?

Last night I dreamt he found me in the field.

The moon sat high.
The waxy leaves silver.

The scythe was gone
and his hands,
when he took mine

felt soft as a child's.

LETTER FROM FOČA

Melica

The one on top set his teeth.

Mama seemed to me
the stronger one even then.

The shutters' slats broke the room into lines
like her fingers
covering my eyes in the street.

Under her the slipcover gathered.
The little roses closed in her fist.

They took their time. They took turns
drinking out of my favorite cup.

(I thought I would eat my tongue.)

The wooden feet of the sofa
creaked against the wooden floor.

And when they decided it was done,
Mama lay as if sleeping

then crossed the room
and beat the door they'd left open

until night came,
until we dreamed that pounding.

THE DREAMER

Kasim

They kept you awake.
Or you just couldn't sleep—such sounds.
Either way, it was the worst part.
You wouldn't think so.
But you can't know such things beforehand.

You dream all the time.
You dream while you're awake.
Sometimes it still happens.
Now, of course, I push it down.
But then, at the time, I'd walk around dreaming.

Not all the dreams were bad.
Sometimes I'd see my old rooster—mean little bastard.
Sometimes I'd see my new stove.
It was new!
Now that was a crime.

You see, I was not a violent man.
But since the camp,
if I had one of theirs in my hands
(even a baby, even a girl)
I'd tear off its arms.

HOPE

Fahra

Jars of fruit I'd dust to keep the tops a gold shine.
Clean windows to let the sun warm the carpets and the wood
and show the dust floating in shoots and streams.
The hush, hush, hush of the broom on the boards.

Hazim playing in the alley. The sweet rise of bread
filling the rooms. Even my mother's low nagging.
It's a song she's teaching me, a song I'll learn.

DRIVING

Boštjan

The line of cars to the border was so long that in the end I decided
to leave mine. I crossed on foot with the old women in
wheelbarrows, the gypsies and cows. Most of them went north
toward Ljubljana or south toward Split. I thought to rest in Venice,
but the stink and sinking made me nervous. So, from Trieste, I took
the bus west.

ANIMALS

Adela

I woke hours before him in the dark
even in summer, to feed the animals
and clean their pens.

I'd leave for the zoo well before dawn
and find him asleep again when I came home.
(We joked our white bed was his other woman.)

Before I left that last time
I looked through the door frame at him
splayed across all of the bed I'd just emptied.

I kissed him goodbye like every day.
His breath was the same, and my hair
smelled already of the zoo—of shit and hay.

That day he tasted as he always did—
new and decayed at once
—like lemon cake, steam, or milk.

CHILD PIECES

Ivana

The houses have taken off their hats.
In winter now it rains and snows
inside the bare rooms.

The kitchen tiles slick with ice
and ash
and sheets of rain.

I tell my children—

> *Alma, Josip.*
> *Get away from there.*

> *Nina, Ivo.*
> *You might fall.*

I tell them
with all the words
I know.
They don't listen anymore.

SOLDIER, BOY

Mufid

I set my back
against a tree
my knife
to peel
a plum

My rifle
lay right
next to me
right next
to me
my gun

When crows
came black
across
the sky
around me
all was green

I did not want
to stand
or sink
I wanted just
to scream

THE DOG

Mehmed

My landlord beats his dog. It's not a bad dog, only untrained and in need of some attention. In the mornings, when I'm drinking my coffee, I can hear him beating it with a stick. The dog whines and barks when he does this. Once my landlord leaves for work it howls. I'm home most of the day. (I'm old. I no longer work, and my back is gone.) Often I walk to meet my friends in the afternoons, the ones who are still alive. We sit in the café and drink coffee and play chess or talk in the park. In spring I can see the dog from my window, chained outside the house, out back. Even asleep in the sun it twitches, as if it dreams of the beatings. I think sometimes it wants me to set it free. Sometimes it looks at me like it's asking.

DEVOTIONAL

Lejla

I can tell you about rain.
The flat scent over the valley, all spring.
It weighed the leaves down.

Our shoes caked with mud. My hair curled.
Dirt turned the boards in the house grey with prints.
Our house, I can tell you, was brick.

My father and uncles built it. Heavy blocks and mortar.
I remember the headscarf I wore the day we moved in.

I was small then.
The new cloth stiff over my ears   and hers.
Fatima.   I remember
our mothers made them to match,

to look like the girl in the picture.
Fata.   Remember.
We took turns on our knees by the window.

MERCY: THE GENERAL

Mlatko

I sat in a tree and watched.
And they bled him anyway.
Father.
My knees were cold.
I remember.
There were sparrows in the leaves around me.

And she. She took her brown hair with her.
Mother,
when the knife came down.
I was small then.
It's what I remember.
She took her brown hair with her.

Now.

My eyes are clear.
Now earth rolls when I say
(and tongues).
Curves over her
and him.

Cowards!

8 o'clock? It's time then.
Now
every hand bends when I say
(at the wrist, at the bone).
I make them. I prove them wrong.

KOSOVO POLJE

The Field of Blackbirds

The blackbirds went mute then flew west
or east—the decided ends of the earth.

First the scarabs
then even the worms found new homes.

Now only crows play in the weeds
or watch from the swinging heads of pines
while men root the dust

for the one thing they claim
will take them back and back and back.

MAKER OF THE BARDAK

Atif

Many of us were potters at the factory in town
—at one time, as many as thirty men.

I've been through other wars,
but now my wife is gone.

I lost her along the Roman road
they marched us out of town on.

LISTMAKER

Nina

The line keeps to the wall then out the door and
around the corner   *One—children three*
      Two alone
      One—wife
This is my post making lists in this book
      with this pen given me You will go
to the border On white paper like so *Children four*
      One girl—alone
You will go from here *Children four* hanging
onto skirts
      One woman—children three
Out the door *Two alone*   eyes
Yes to the right *One*   *grown*   soiled   No room
      One old   for baskets
      One son   or pets
Yes none No dogs *One woman*   fat hands
      In the truck   *—alone*
      Your things will be returned
Rope belt   Yes At the border I tell them
      Yes   I have children   Four
of my own   Ink   hair Yes There

THE SAVA

Goran

When the river rises or begins to rise, we as neighbors, as men,
gather the sandbags kept at the Community Center and pass them
down the avenue, one at a time, down the main street of town, man
to man, to the edge of the rising water.

The bags push the water and raging earth back into itself like folds
of dough or batter. There have been times, my father tells me of
two he can remember, when the rains loosed so much soil that the
banks and the bags gave way. The sand burst its burlap casings and
became part of the water, the flood, the Sava, leaving us here
in boats to watch the tops of our houses pass—roofs, chimneys,
picture frames.

THE LAST DAY

Zehra

It rained all week.
It rained all spring.
      But not this day.

Water clung to our skin
      —but this day was clear.
And the wind heaved a wet world
      down from heaven—but this day was dry.

All week it rained. It pried us
      like roses in the garden.
But not this day.
      No rain. No sun. This day—dry thorn.

On this day the blooms sealed.
On this day they took him.

THE MUSIC TEACHER

Osman

The boys who came to take me had been my pupils.
I taught them Beethoven.
They could not meet my eyes.

Instead they waited:
Shuffle. Rifle. Dirty hair.

I packed my bag:
Scores. Spit. Diploma.

Forty miles to Travnik—I joined the walking.
Trucks passed carrying men
I knew not to envy.

MY SENA

Behta

In the afternoon she'd come back to me
covered in the smell of fruit,
shoes clotted with dirt.
She'd kick them off at the door
no matter how I scolded her.

The sun came and went.
The dust settled around the house.
(Even the dust was sweet with Sena.)

She was a child in the orchard
at her grandfather's heels.
With the years her movements slowed.

With her eyes she took the world apart in pieces,
pieces she held for a moment then set down.

A GLOSSARY: THE LIVES OF A GIRL

Senada

Ašikovanje	courtship
ašikovanti	court
bašča	garden
berićet	divine blessing or fortune
cura	unmarried girl or (unmarried) young woman
curica	little girl
fildžan	small coffee cup without a handle
gatanje	fotune-telling
igranka	dance
komšija	neighbor
merhaba	informal Muslim greeting
momak	bachelor, young man
pendžer	window
pogača	type of bread (flat and round)
radost	joy
sabah	dawn, morning
sabah	morning prayers
sekirati	worry
šerbe	sweet drink made of sugar and water, rosewater or fruit juice
sevdah	love
sihir	sorcery
šljiva	plum
sramota	shame
stećak	tombstone with specific decorations, dating from the middle ages
svadba	wedding
svatovi	wedding guests, wedding procession
svekr	husband's father
svekra	husband's mother
tabut	lidless coffin
tespih	prayer beads
uda se	to marry (of a woman)

ukrala se	marriage by elopement (said of a girl)
ureći nekoga	to cast a spell on someone
vjernik	believer
zikir	remembrance of the names of God

PARIS

Emina

I didn't want to go.
But at the first signs of trouble
my parents packed our bags.
Alone, together
at the border my brothers went missing.
The men there made me go on with the train
alone. I stay here now
with cousins near the Bastille.
There's a monument.
From the apartment window I can . . .
Yes, near the Opera.
There's a monument.
You know it?
My parents said they'd join me in the spring.
We'd listen to Puccini
and drink champagne
on the day I turned nineteen.
They said:
This is as it should be.
I work.
Yes, folding laundry,
and stop here at six each day to smoke
and take a glass of beer.
Lately the light is yellow.
Summer light in Paris.
Yes, it's fine. Cold, as it should be.

BREAD LINE

Hasan

Our shoes are stiff for winter although it's spring.
Inside the leather our feet press down.   Bones to the hard earth.
My hunger feeds my thirst.   (Its burning spreads like sleep.)
Believing it will end soon   I close my eyes standing
and say nothing to my friends. Lead fingers   at the ends of my palms.
Lead hands.   Days and nights we wait in line.
We taste the bread that never comes.
This is the torturer's tongue
passing over us   here
as in our homes.   Through doorways or windows
through walls.   Through the miles of my childhood I keep close.
I've made a map of   its routes   I trace in my pocket
as always   when I'm cold.
Doesn't this night seem darker than any in winter?
And isn't it May?   Now
a young man plays   among us in line.
And on his strings   hands like horses.
I remember   this song
but not   its end.

THE BRIDGE

THE BRIDGE

Vladimir

Between you and me
I sweep the houses clean.
With just this yellow straw,
this one broom. I do it
so the others can move in.

I tell you
the floor of this house is a hundred floors.
This house, I tell you,
is a hundred houses,
more.

To pass the time I watch the broom
rake lines in the dust. I sing songs
or look over their things:

      Pictures, books, children's toys.
No TV sets. No VCRs.
      These were taken first, of course.

And sometimes, between us,
I stop my work and weigh my palm in my palm.

So light.
I think.
What could I have done, one man?

THE BRIDGE

The Bridge

I held your feet before you dove
and kissed the green and foaming waters.

I watched your mouths slack—tongues free
finally of the need to speak.

Once carts crossed my back
and the clip, clop, clip, clop
clip, clop, clip, clop.

Then rubber tires.
Then stories from the hills.

He furnished them for truth—that crested one of you.

It's not for him.
It's not for you.

It lives in the stones below the river
—white granite blocks carry you over.

THE BRIDGE

The Stones, The Water

one man, one man
one man, one man
   one man, one man
       one man, one man
   one man, one man
one man, one man
one man, one man
   one man, one man
       one man, one man
   one man, one man
one man, one man
one man, one man
   one man, one man
       one man, one man
   one man, one man
one man, one man
one man, one man
   one man, one man
       one man, one man
   one man, one man
one man, one man
one man, one man
   one man, one man
       one man, one man
   one man, one man
one man, one man
one man, one man
   one man, one man
       one man, one man
   one man, one man
one man, one man
one man, one man
   one man, one man

one man, one man
one man, one man
one man, one man
one man, one man
one man, one man
one man, one man
one man, one man
one man, one man
one man, one man
one man, one man
one man, one man
one man, one man
one man, one man
one man, one man
one man, one man
one man, one man
one man, one man
one man, one man
one man, one man
one man, one man
one man, one man
one man, one man
one man, one man
one man, one man
one man, one man
one man, one man
one man, one man
one man, one man
one man, one man
one man, one man

FIELDS

NETTLES

Fatima

The guns have become.
The guns have become like friends.
Blunt comfort we steel our thumbs.
The guns have become mettle right.

The chairs.
The chairs we choose to leave alone.
With desks and heels riveted down.
Riveted dumb.
Like children.
The chairs we sit in or move from.

And underneath.
What's gone.
Wink of teeth.
Clap of sun.
Is gone.

MOTHER TONGUE

Neda

My son sleeps long in the morning.
It's only then that I recognize him.

Words are a train I chase, I chase
through flat blue fields.

No!

    The words for *my* son
are the leaves on the trees
    the train passes and ignores.

They sing stinging songs in my grandmother's
grandmother's voice.

    Hiccups.
        High laughs. Wheezes . . .

Like wind through a wire fence.
A bird's narrow lung.

LAMENT

Dino

I loved her.
And he was
My friend.
I pulled   the trigger.
And it was
His end.

NAMES

Salim

When we lose
Our houses
Like bets.
When we sleep
In cots
In camps
Our names
Fall away
Like dreams.
Our names
Dissolve
Into water
Like sugar
Into air
Like breath.
They empty
Into mattresses
Sweet
With filth
Into pots
Of thin soup.
The nearest
Of God's
Places.
We lose
Our names
Our houses.

TIGER

Janko

I haven't seen Vesna in twelve weeks.
She gave me a tape of my favorite songs
to listen to on my headphones.

> *Love, love me do . . .*

Today I was out of sorts.
I had only two hours' sleep
and five cigarettes.

> *You know I love you . . .*

I try to exercise, even here.
There's always something you can find to lift
—bricks, cans of fuel.

> *I'll always be true . . .*

I write to tell her:
Wait for me.
I'll be home soon.

SOLDIER, GIRL

Alisa

I became a tree when he chased me.
I became a tree when he chased me.

He ran through and soaked me skin and root.
In the cool wet earth like wax in the water I was brittle.
(Not like the vines that took up in the wind.)

> Years before the white moon sat low over my house.
> My family under its roof.

I could have stayed all summer there
under that moon—but the black sky behind her.
Yes.
> Instead,
> I became this.

A winter of sound.
I became a tree when he chased me
then chopped, chopped, chopped down.

HIDING

Nita

We kept the basement dark.
Light hook in eye. Bridge of oil.

One smell I remember—burn
—yellow smell of hiding.

My father kept the lamp to drink
and use until . . .

and so, one hand I oil.
And dark ring find.
So bridge.
So hook in eye.

LULLABY

Dragan

The wind was always cold, a draft
In mother's dumbing mouth.
We ate and drank and shat and slept,
But none of it ever enough.

> Fuck. Fuck. There is a drum in me.
> Spit. Spit. You cunt for luck.

> Hand over the legs and arms and toes.
> Hand over the budding crook.

These forty rings a rosary
All on my arm still burn.
My father held a suckling pig
For me to take my turn.

> Fuck. Fuck. There is a dam in me.
> Cut. Cut. You cunt for luck.

> Hand over the nails and eyes and brows.
> Hand over the wine to suck.

We never spoke, we'd only work,
And working was the test.
And gasoline, it filled our lungs.
Its shadow our bitter guest.

> Fuck. Fuck. There is a dam in me.
> A drum, you cunt, you crook.

> Hand over the nails and eyes and tongues,
>   the brows, the breasts, the teeth and lungs.
> Hand over the lids of eyes and palms.
>   And cover your ears for shock.

A PLACE CALLED SREBRENICA: THE HANGED GIRL

I just can't say
I just can't
say—just Not   to go alone

With no shoes on.
She climbed a high tree
near the muddy ditch.
Knotting a shabby floral shawl
her head of black hair through it leapt.

"What am I supposed to tell her?
Why is this happening
and we're not doing anything?"

(Not to go alone   to go alone)

EPILOGUE

MY NAME IS ALMA

Alma

The women carry my arms
or I lean on the plaster.
I watch the window (wooden hands)
hold yellow birds. They fly through.

I sit on my bed. Listening. Listen.
I live in the skin. My bones are glass,
are mirrors, are my brothers,
are mouths that speak in my sleep.

The women feed me pills and eggs
to shine the glass but not the mirrors.
They want me to tell them
my name but not my brothers.'

And not the birds. Or the sky
that holds them. Not their names.
Never the ones my bones speak,
mouths open in sleep.

Though the following notes on individual poems make reference to only a handful of texts, all of the books listed following the notes, in various ways, were essential to my understanding of the history and nature of the war in Bosnia and the former Yugoslavia.

THE NATIONAL LIBRARY: The National Library in Sarajevo was bombed on August 25, 1992.

PAPA'S DREAM: Bairam is a Bosnian Muslim holiday. There are, in fact, two of these holidays with the same name. In the more elaborately celebrated of the two, a lamb is killed for roasting. This Bairam falls near Easter, and before the war Catholics would often bring their Muslim neighbors decorated eggs to share their celebration. Tone Bringa, *Being Muslim the Bosnian Way: Identity and Community in a Central Bosnian Village* (Princeton, N. J.: Princeton Univ. Press, 1995), 78.

Covering the hair with a head scarf is traditional among older rural Bosnian women of all backgrounds (63). In addition, wearing glass charms, carrying some kind of knife or sword (especially an iron one), and avoiding the use of a person's name are all traditional Balkan ways of warding off evil or seeking protection from it. Mary E. Durham, *Some Tribal Origins, Laws, and Customs of the Balkans* (New York: Macmillan, 1929), 289, 296, 297, 302.

"Kahva" is "coffee" in Bosnian. "Tiho" is "quiet."

WATER: This poem in general was inspired by (and the character Asim, in particular, is drawn from) Christopher Merrill, *Only the Nails Remain: Scenes from the Balkan Wars* (Lanham, Md.: Rowman and Littlefield, 1999), xvii–xviii, 43.

ZLATA ON THE OUTSIDE: The Zlata in this poem refers to Zlata Filopović, whose diary, *Zlata's Diary: A Child's Life in Sarajevo*, became a best-seller.

BURYING TITO: Josip Broz Tito was the founder of communist Yugoslavia. He ruled from 1945 until his death in 1980. In many village homes in Bosnia-Herzegovina, his picture could be found in the foyer or living room. Bringa, *Being Muslim the Bosnian Way*, 8–9. Despite the fact that his rule was repressive, Tito was much respected for having brought peace and relative prosperity to Yugoslavia.

THE TEACHER: The Slobo in this poem is Slobodan Milošević.

CARNIVAL: The lines Sabiha reads in this poem are from Robert Fagles, "The Sack of Troy," in *The Greek Myths* (New York: Penguin, 1992), 698.

DEVOTIONAL: "The girl in the picture" refers to the popular image of a Muslim girl in a headscarf praying on her knees that could often be found in Bosnian Muslim households. Bringa, *Being Muslim the Bosnian Way*, 8.

MERCY: THE GENERAL: Though Mlatko is fictional, his character is based on both the former Serbian president Slobodan Milošević, whose mother committed suicide when he was a child, and General Blagoje Adžić, who watched from a tree in his village as his family were killed by Ustaše (Croatian Nazi sympathizers) during World War II. Peter Maass, *Love Thy Neighbor: A Story of War* (New York: Vintage, 1996), 38.

KOSOVO POLJE: At Kosovo Polje in 1389, the Serb people lost a battle that ushered in over five hundred years of oppressive Ottoman rule in the region. The battle and the place (the battlefield is known as the Field of Blackbirds) are revered in Serbian folklore and history. ("The myth of Kosovo is the centerpiece of the Serbian tradition.") Laura Silber and Allan Little, *Yugoslavia: Death of a Nation* (New York: Penguin, 1997), 72. In 1989 Slobodan Milošević spoke at a celebration of the six-hundredth anniversary of the battle. This speech was among his most potent calls to arms.

MAKER OF THE BARDAK: Before running water was installed in most mosques, a *bardak*, a clay pitcher whose design dates back to the Roman Empire, was used to cleanse the hands and feet before entering the mosque to pray. (The bardak was also used for various household functions.) They were common in pre–World War II Bosnia and are no longer produced for use. Bringa, *Being Muslim the Bosnian Way*, 88.

LISTMAKER: During the war, Bosnian Muslims regularly were forced from their homes, rounded up and killed, or taken (often by truck) either to concentration camps or beyond the borders of their hometowns, where they would be killed. Men of fighting age and boys were usually separated from girls, women, and the elderly.

THE SAVA: The Sava is a river that runs from the north through Slovenia, then along the border between Bosnia and Croatia, and finally into what was Serbia and is now Yugoslavia. Sava Nemanjić was also the name of the founder of the Serbian Orthodox Church.

THE MUSIC TEACHER: When the central Bosnian city of Jajce was bombed relentlessly by Serb nationalists (October 1992), some thirty thousand of its residents fled toward the relative safety of the city of

Travnik, forty miles over mountains and rough roads. Many of these people died along the way. The character in this poem was inspired in part by an account of a man Peter Maass interviewed in Travnik. Maass, *Love Thy Neighbor*, 99.

A GLOSSARY: THE LIVES OF A GIRL: Translations found in Bringa, *Being Muslim the Bosnian Way*, 253–57.

BREAD LINE: On May 27, 1992, twenty-two Sarajevans were killed while waiting in line for bread. Scores more were injured in an incident that became known as the "breadline massacre." On May 28 at the site of the blast, Vedran Smailović, principal cellist of the Sarajevo Opera Orchestra, began to play Albinoni's Adagio in G Minor, a piece which had been found in ruined Dresden after World War II. Smailovic played for twenty-two consecutive days in memoriam.

THE BRIDGE: Made of twelve arches of white granite, the bridge being referred to in all three of the poems in this section is the famous bridge over the Drina River in the southeastern Bosnian town of Višegrad. The bridge lies near the border of Bosnia and Serbia. It was a primary trade route for centuries and is considered by many to be a symbol of the meeting of two cultures, of East and West, and the passage between them. Many atrocities were committed on the bridge during this and previous wars.

During the war in Bosnia, the town of Višegrad was "cleansed" of its Muslim population; their homes were looted, and their mosques were leveled. The speaker in the first poem is based on Vladimir Radjen, a middle-aged Bosnian-Serb man who was interviewed in Maass, *Love Thy Neighbor*, 11.

The Bridge on the Drina, the title of Nobel Prize Laureate Ivo Andić's epic novel, refers to this same bridge.

TIGER: The Tigers were an infamous and particularly brutal Serb militia.

A PLACE CALLED SREBRENICA: Srebrenica was a UN "safe area" that fell to Serb nationalist forces in July 1995. The massacre that occurred there was the largest single incident of mass murder on European soil since the Holocaust. NATO troops who had promised to protect the people of Srebrenica did nothing to stop it.

The lines in italics draw on a *Washington Post* article by John Promfret. The story included a photograph of a girl who'd hanged herself from a tree after surviving the massacre at Srebrenica. The lines in quotes in the next stanza refer to comments made by Vice President Al Gore to President Bill Clinton and others during a cabinet meeting. His comments refer to Promfret's story and the situation in Bosnia in general. Gore refers to his daughter in the first quoted line. Samantha Power, *"A Problem from Hell": America and the Age of Genocide* (New York: Basic, 2002), 413.

Many of the voices and ideas in the pages of the following books inspired those in *Rooms and Fields:*

Andrić, Ivo. *The Bridge on the Drina.* Chicago: Univ. of Chicago Press, 1984.

Bringa, Tone. *Being Muslim the Bosnian Way: Identity and Community in a Central Bosnian Village.* Princeton, N.J.: Princeton Univ. Press, 1995.

Drakulić, Slavenka. *The Balkan Express: Fragments from the Other Side of War.* New York: Norton, 1993.

Durham, Mary E. *Some Tribal Origins, Laws, and Customs of the Balkans.* New York: Macmillan, 1929.

Fagles, Robert. *The Greek Myths.* New York: Penguin, 1992.

Filipović, Zlata. *Zlata's Diary: A Child's Life in Sarajevo.* New York: Penguin, 1995.

Glenny, Misha, *The Fall of Yugoslavia: The Third Balkan War.* New York: Penguin, 1993.

Haviv, Ron. *Blood and Honey: A Balkan War Journal.* New York: TV Books/ Umbrage, 2000.

Maass, Peter. *Love Thy Neighbor: A Story of War.* New York: Vintage, 1996.

Merrill, Christopher. *Only the Nails Remain: Scenes from the Balkan Wars.* Lanham, Md.: Rowman and Littlefield, 1999.

Power, Samantha. *"A Problem from Hell": America and the Age of Genocide.* New York: Basic, 2002.

Sacco, Joe. *Safe Area Goražde: The War in Eastern Bosnia, 1992–1995.* Seattle, Wash.: Fantagraphics, 2000.

Sells, Michael A. *The Bridge Betrayed: Religion and Genocide in Bosnia.* Berkeley: Univ. of California Press, 1996.

Silber, Laura, and Allan Little. *Yugoslavia: Death of a Nation.* New York: Penguin, 1997.

Stiglmayer, Alexandra, ed. *Mass Rape: The War against Women in Bosnia-Herzegovina.* Lincoln: Univ. of Nebraska Press, 1994.

Žarkovi, Radmila Manojlović, ed. *I Remember / Sjećam Se: Writings by Bosnian Women Refugees.* San Francisco: Aunt Lute Books, 1996.

ACKNOWLEDGMENTS

My brief time at the Vermont Studio Center was essential to this book's completion and propulsion. Great thanks to all the people I was so lucky to encounter there, in particular Lorraine Mainelli, Alison Horvitz, and J. J. Hanson.

Thanks also to Vince Gotera, Susan Terris, Francine Ringold, and all the editors of the following publications in which a number of poems from this series first appeared:

The *North American Review*, "Letter from Foča"; *Runes*, "My Name Is Alma"; *Nimrod International Journal*, "Breadline," "The National Library," and "Scavenger's Daughter"; *Comstock Review*, "Water"; and *Seattle Review*, "Hope."

I am forever indebted to my dear friend and traveling companion, Saša Pustovrh, and to her family, for picking me up in Germany, for the use of the car and the map, and for their tremendous hospitality. To the lovely Munira Oković, a very special and heartfelt thanks, for her help as translator, friend, and assistant. Thanks too to her family here and in Bosnia and to all the people who so generously shared their stories with me. Finally, warm thanks, as well, to Mirsad Sijarić for all the eleventh-hour e-mail aid.

My deepest gratitude goes to my husband, my first reader, my friend, Jonathan Wei, for his unwavering support of this book and me. Unending thanks to Jean Valentine for selecting and believing in these poems and to Suzanne Gardinier for setting me to the chase. Praise and thanks to Maggie Anderson for her guidance and patience and to Alice Cone for her humor and all her help.

Finally, I owe profound thanks and gratitude to the rest of my family and friends, especially my grandmother, Dorothy Peterson, and my parents, Karen McLean and Steven Peterson. And to Barbara Littenberg, Armando Sosa, Kent Peterson, Miriam Peterson, Beatrice Landolt, Ulka Sachdev, Michelle Valladares, Kyes Stevens, Patrick Rosal, Curtis Bauer and Andrea Hornick, thank you for everything.